# United Nations –
# *Peacekeeper?*

# Edward Johnson

**Global Issues Series**

Closing the Borders
Genetic Engineering
The Rich-Poor Divide
Terrorism
United Nations – Peacekeeper?
Violence in Society

Editor: Merle Thompson
Series Editor: Cath Senker
Designer: Simon Borrough

First published in 1995 by Wayland (Publishers) Ltd, 61 Western Road, Hove, East Sussex BN3 1JD, England

**British Library Cataloguing in Publication Data**
Johnson, Edward
United Nations: Peacekeeper? – (Global Issues series)
I. Title II Series
327.172
ISBN 0 7502 1172 5

Typeset by Simon Borrough
Printed and bound by G. Canale C.S.p.A., Turin, Italy

Cover picture: A Norwegian soldier from the United Nations Interim Force in Lebanon (UNIFIL) on duty at an observation post in southern Lebanon. UNIFIL was created in 1978 to help to restore peace and security in Lebanon, and to make sure that Israeli troops had withdrawn from the area.

Title page picture: A member of the UN force in the Congo (now Zaire), in 1960, helps a small victim of the civil war.

**Picture Acknowledgements**

Camera Press title page (T. Spencer), 8, 10, 11, 12 (L. Skoogfors), 14, 15, 20 (J.Haillot/L'Express), 21 (Israel Sun), 41, 48 (Benoit Gysembergh), 49 (Fiona McDougall), 53 (Benoit Gysembergh), 54 (Gavin Smith), 55 (Benoit Gysembergh); Topham 9 (R. Frehm), 13, 17, 24, 25, 29, 30, 31, 33, 36 (S. Lyon/STF), 37 (P. Northall), 40, 44 (E. F. Marti), 45 (S. Ratkovic), 52 (H. Krauss); United Nations cover (141245/ J. Isaac), 6, 7, 16, 18, 19, 22 (Y. Nagata), 23 (M. Tzovaras), 26 (161894/Saw Lwin), 27 (156744/M. Grant), 29 (157214/ M. Grant), 32 (157089), 34 (159185/P. Sudhakaran), 35 (159456/P. Sudhakaran), 38 (159301/J. Isaac), 39 (159283/ J. Isaac), 42 (159301/J. Isaac), 43 (182009/M. Tzovaras), 50 (182120), 51 (159384/M. Grant), 56 (135526), 57 (186266), 58 (87491), 59 (174139).

# CONTENTS

Map: United Nations peacekeeping and
  observer forces since 1945     **4**
Introduction     **6**
Enforcing peace     **8**
Peacekeeping – calming combatants     **16**
Peacekeeping – assisting transition     **26**
Peacekeeping – moderating civil wars     **36**
Peacekeeping – controlling civil wars     **48**
Conclusion     **56**
Glossary     **61**
Books to read     **62**
List of United Nations peacekeeping
  and observer forces since 1945     **62**
Index     **63**

# United Nations peacekeeping

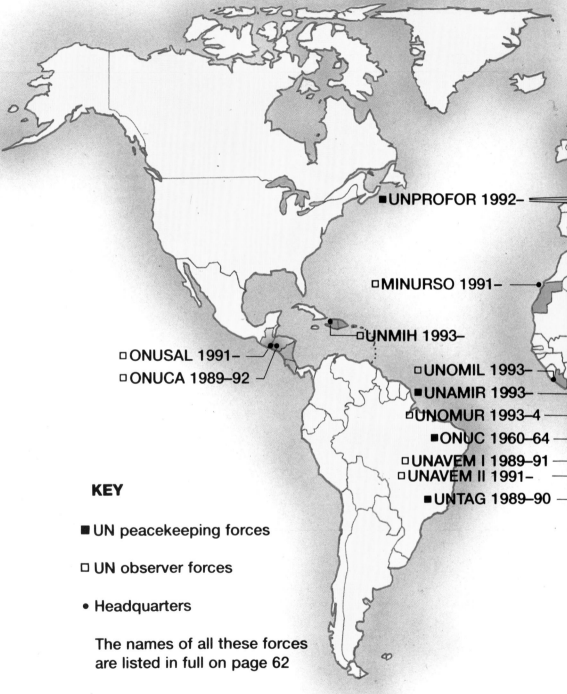

■UNPROFOR 1992–

□MINURSO 1991–

□UNMIH 1993–

□ONUSAL 1991–
□ONUCA 1989–92

□UNOMIL 1993–
■UNAMIR 1993–
□UNOMUR 1993–4
■ONUC 1960–64
□UNAVEM I 1989–91
□UNAVEM II 1991–
■UNTAG 1989–90

**KEY**

■ UN peacekeeping forces

□ UN observer forces

• Headquarters

The names of all these forces
are listed in full on page 62

# and observer forces since 1945

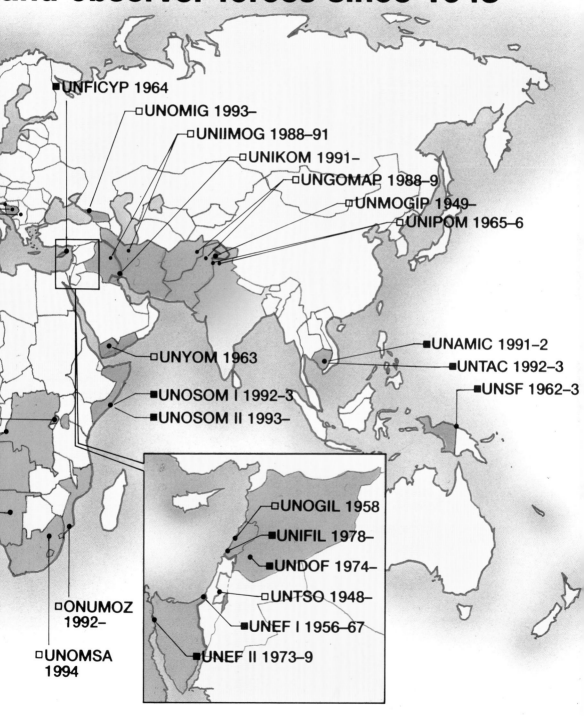

- ■ UNFICYP 1964
- □ UNOMIG 1993–
- □ UNIIMOG 1988–91
- □ UNIKOM 1991–
- □ UNGOMAP 1988–9
- □ UNMOGIP 1949–
- □ UNIPOM 1965–6
- ■ UNAMIC 1991–2
- ■ UNTAC 1992–3
- ■ UNSF 1962–3
- □ UNYOM 1963
- ■ UNOSOM I 1992–3
- ■ UNOSOM II 1993–
- □ ONUMOZ 1992–
- □ UNOMSA 1994

Inset:
- □ UNOGIL 1958
- ■ UNIFIL 1978–
- ■ UNDOF 1974–
- □ UNTSO 1948–
- ■ UNEF I 1956–67
- ■ UNEF II 1973–9

# INTRODUCTION

In 1945, at the end of the Second World War, the victorious powers of the USA, Britain and the Soviet Union came together to take the lead in forming the United Nations Organization (UN). This body now includes almost all the states throughout the world among its members. Its main purpose is the maintenance of world peace and the avoidance of war.

Since the UN was created, however, there have been numerous wars across the globe, resulting in millions of casualties. It might seem that the UN has not been very successful in bringing peace to the world.

In 1949, members of the UN General Assembly are addressed by the US President, Harry S. Truman, during the ceremony of the laying of the cornerstone of the UN's permanent headquarters, in New York.

Harry S. Truman addresses the delegates from fifty nations attending the San Francisco Conference in 1945. The UN was set up during this conference.

Yet, the UN can only do what its members and, in particular, the major powers allow it to do. The failure to end war between nations has not really been the fault of the UN. It is more the fault of states that have tried to find solutions to their problems through war and violence, rather than through peaceful means. Despite its failures, the UN has provided some useful services to a number of communities, through the work of its peacekeeping forces. The UN soldiers and police, in their distinctive blue berets and white vehicles, have, since the late 1980s, become very familiar in trouble spots throughout the world.

UN peacekeepers have patrolled borders between hostile states; monitored elections and assisted states to reach independence; distributed humanitarian aid and tried to calm, and even control, civil wars. These are only some of the wide range of roles performed by UN peacekeepers, but these are the roles we shall look at in this book.

‘ ’

• • •

In 1946, the British Prime Minister, Clement Attlee, said that the aim of those setting up the United Nations was
‘... not just the negation [abolition] of war, but the creation of a world of security and freedom, of a world which is governed by justice and the moral law. We desire to assert the pre-eminence of right over might and the general good against selfish and sectional aims.’

# ENFORCING PEACE

In 1945, the founders of the UN expected that the organization would maintain international peace by the very fact that countries would be working together, as allies, within it. If fighting did break out, the intention was that the major powers (the Soviet Union, the United States of America, Britain, France and Nationalist China), which were all permanent members of the UN Security Council, would act together to stop the conflict. If necessary, the UN would intervene with armed forces to restore international peace and security. It was anticipated, therefore, that the UN would have forces of its own which it could send to a trouble spot to stop the fighting by military action. This would result in the enforcement of peace by the UN whenever necessary.

The UN Security Council (right) debates the crisis that arose in the Gulf, after Iraq invaded Kuwait in 1991.

Missiles on show at a Soviet military parade (below). The staging of parades such as these showed the extent of the distrust and hostility between the major powers during the Cold War. This tense atmosphere hindered the workings of the UN.

**FACT FILE**

**The Security Council and the power of veto**
The most important body in the UN is the Security Council. At present, it has fifteen members, five of which are permanent members. These five permanent members are called the P5 and now consist of the USA, Russia, Britain, France and China. The other members of the Security Council serve for two years and are elected by the General Assembly, which is made up of representatives from all member states of the UN. One important difference between the P5 and the non-permanent members is that each of the P5 has a veto. This means that if any one of them votes against a resolution made in the Security Council it cannot be adopted.

However, the UN quickly ran into difficulties. Relations among the major powers, particularly the USA and Britain on the one side, and the Soviet Union on the other, worsened once the Second World War was over and the Axis Powers (Germany, Italy and Japan) had been defeated. There were many disagreements, and these countries, which had once been allies, sunk into a deeply hostile relationship that, while it did not lead to open warfare, was sufficiently frosty to be termed the Cold War.

The UN was badly affected by the worsening relations among the major powers as the Cold War developed, and it was never given the responsibility, or the armed force that it was supposed to have, to enforce international peace. Instead, the two opposing blocs in the Cold War developed their own means of maintaining security in the areas under their influence, through the North Atlantic Treaty Organization (NATO) and the Warsaw Pact. The UN was left on the sidelines, and its authority became weakened, as it could do little to establish peace in the face of divisions between the USA and the Soviet Union. This was particularly the case when the two superpowers supported different sides in any conflict, especially in parts of Africa and Asia. The UN was kept from intervening in events by the superpowers which sought peace on their own terms.

There have, however, been two instances of the enforcement of peace where the UN has supported direct military action, but these have been the exception rather than the rule. In both cases, the superpower opposition to enforcement was removed: in the first case by chance, and in the second as a result of the ending of the Cold War and the improved relations between the superpowers after 1989. The first case was during the Korean War, fought from 1950 to 1953. The second was in the Gulf War, through Operation Desert Storm, in 1991.

US troops, as part of the UN army, capture a North Korean position.

A US soldier (right) interrogates a North Korean nurse during the Korean War. US forces played the major role in the military operations which were approved by the UN Security Council.

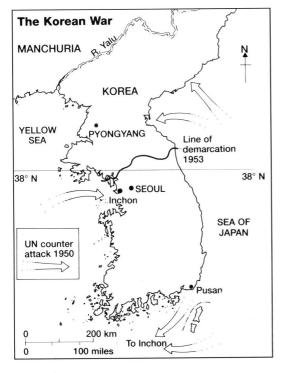

## The Korean War

MANCHURIA

R. Yalu

KOREA

N

PYONGYANG

YELLOW SEA

Line of demarcation 1953

38° N                              38° N

SEOUL

Inchon

SEA OF JAPAN

UN counter attack 1950

Pusan

0          200 km

0          100 miles

To Inchon

FACT FILE

### The Korean War

After the defeat of the Japanese forces in 1945, at the end of the Second World War, Korea was occupied jointly for a short time by the USA in the south and by the Soviet Union in the north. In 1947, a UN Commission was sent to supervise free elections, but was not allowed to enter the northern part of the country which was controlled by the Communists. In South Korea, the people elected a government headed by President Syngman Rhee, while in North Korea, Kim Il Sung was proclaimed leader. Both governments claimed the right to control the whole country.

After the invasion by the North Korean army in 1950, the UN army found itself pushed right back to the southern tip of the country. Gradually, the UN troops managed to force the North Koreans up to the Chinese border. The military success of the UN army led China, which had turned Communist in 1949, to enter the war on the side of the North Koreans. Together, the North Koreans and the Chinese Communists forced the UN troops to retreat south. The fighting reached a stalemate at the 38th parallel (latitude 38° N). Both sides signed an armistice agreement and the forces remained facing each other, as they still do to this day.

In June 1950, the army of the Communist government of North Korea crossed the border and invaded South Korea. The UN Security Council declared North Korea to be an aggressor and approved a force made up of troops from fifteen states to intervene on behalf of the South Korean government. However, the UN was only able to authorize this force because the Soviet Union had temporarily withdrawn from the UN Security Council at the time, and therefore could not state its opposition to the UN action and use its power of veto. The action in Korea was peace enforcement, but it was carried out with a force that was not, strictly, a UN force, and the circumstances were unusual. It is more helpful to think of the UN action in the Korean War as an operation led by the USA which used the UN as a means of gaining support for its actions. The UN operation in Korea was not paid for from UN funds, and the force received its orders from the US-appointed military commander, not the UN Secretary General. There is no doubt that, had the Soviet Union been able to use its veto, the UN would not have approved this action.

Bomb damage in Iraq (right) caused by the coalition forces during Operation Desert Storm, in 1991. Iraqi civilians inspect a huge bomb crater which has filled with water.

## The Gulf War

This example of peace enforcement in Korea, from the early days of the Cold War, was unusual, and the UN had to wait until the Cold War had ended before it was able to authorize such action again.

US troops training in the desert before the beginning of Operation Desert Storm.

In August 1990, the Iraqi army crossed over the border into Kuwait and illegally occupied the country. The USA felt this invasion threatened both the US and the world economy, which depended on cheap and reliable supplies of oil. It organized a loose coalition of nearly thirty states, through the UN, to oppose Iraq, politically and militarily. Russia (which retained the seat on the Security Council formerly belonging to the Soviet Union) was broadly prepared to go along with this and allow the UN to give its 'stamp of approval' to the US action.

FACT FILE

**The invasion of Kuwait**
Iraq had a long-standing claim to Kuwait, which is rich in oil. The immediate dispute between the two states arose because Kuwait was selling its oil too cheaply on the world market. This undercut Iraq's oil price. It was important for Iraq to keep the price of oil high as it needed the money from its sale to rebuild the country after its war with Iran from 1980 to 1988.

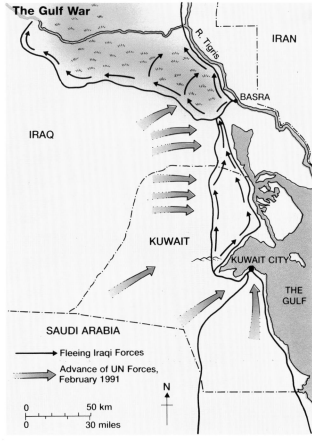

**The Gulf War**

IRAN

R. Tigris

BASRA

IRAQ

KUWAIT

KUWAIT CITY

THE GULF

SAUDI ARABIA

→ Fleeing Iraqi Forces

⇒ Advance of UN Forces, February 1991

N

0      50 km
0      30 miles

The USA was able to steer twelve resolutions against Iraq's occupation of Kuwait through the UN Security Council, and the Soviet Union supported all of them. The most significant of these was Resolution 678 of 29 November 1990. In this, the UN Security Council authorized the coalition of states to use force if Iraq had not withdrawn its troops from Kuwait by 15 January 1991.

### Operation Desert Storm

As a result of Resolution 678, the US government was able to organize a large military force to carry out an operation called Desert Storm. The Iraqi army was defeated and driven out of Kuwait. While most of the troops and equipment for this operation came from the USA, there were major contributions from France and Britain. In addition, before the land battle was actually fought, the allies carried out a long bombing campaign against Iraq, from military airfields in Turkey and in Arab states belonging to the coalition.

Iraqi troops in Kuwait surrender to coalition forces on the second day of Operation Desert Storm, February 1991.

However, as with the peace enforcement action in Korea, the military operation was not paid for by the UN, and the political decisions surrounding it were made, not by the UN Secretary General, but by the US government. The main financial supporters of Operation Desert Storm were the Arab states opposed to Iraq, particularly Saudi Arabia and other countries such as Japan and Germany.

Military decisions were made by US military commanders, appointed by the US President not by the UN Secretary General. The Security Council had no control over the operation once Resolution 678 had been passed by the UN.

In Korea and the Gulf War, peace enforcement through the UN was possible because, for different reasons, the USA and the Soviet Union, and later Russia, did not block each other in the UN. In the case of Korea, it was purely by accident that the Soviet Union was not in a position to oppose the USA. In the case of the Gulf War, the ending of the Cold War in 1989 had produced better relations between the USA and Russia and a desire to co-operate more closely in the UN.

Kuwaiti women celebrating the victory of the coalition forces against Iraq and the liberation of their country. They are carrying Kuwaiti flags and pictures of the ruler of Kuwait who was then still in exile.

# PEACEKEEPING – CALMING COMBATANTS

As the Cold War prevented the UN from being able to enforce peace in the way it had originally hoped, it looked for other ways in which it might be able to intervene in conflicts to assist the creation of peace. The UN was able to organize two small, unarmed observer forces to help to create stability, one in the Middle East in 1948, and another, a year later, in Kashmir. These small forces were to provide models for UN peacekeeping operations to follow in the future.

## The Suez crisis

The second UN Secretary General, Dag Hammarskjold (1953–61), saw an opportunity for UN action during the Suez Crisis of 1956. In that year, British, French and Israeli armed forces had invaded Egypt, but had been forced to end the fighting and to withdraw, because of diplomatic and economic pressure from the USA and world opinion.

## The United Nations Emergency Force (UNEF)

Against this background, the UN General Assembly asked Hammarskjold to organize UNEF, a small UN force made up of soldiers from ten countries. This force was sent to Egypt to supervise the withdrawal of the invading armies from Egyptian territory. It then moved on to the Egyptian–Israeli border where it observed the cease-fire between the two states, guarded essential installations, and reported on border incidents.

UN military observers in Kashmir, as part of the United Nations Military Observer Group in India and Pakistan (UNMOGIP). At this time, UN forces did not wear their distinctive blue berets.

### Suez

In 1956, the Egyptian government, under President Nasser, nationalized the Suez Canal Company, which controlled the operation of the Canal through Egyptian territory. The British and French governments, which part-owned the Canal, were opposed to this action. They wished to see Nasser removed and the Canal placed, once again, under international ownership. However, the USA did not wish to see force used in the Middle East, nor to see Nasser overthrown.

As a way around the US position, the British and French joined with the Israeli government in a highly secret plan. Israel invaded Egypt and advanced towards the Canal. At this point, the British and French issued an ultimatum to both Israel and Egypt to stop fighting. The Israelis, as planned, called a halt but Egypt did not. The British and French then invaded Egypt.

There seems no doubt that, during its eleven-year stay, from 1956 to 1967, UNEF helped to keep peace in the Middle East. Its presence on the Egyptian–Israeli border discouraged either side from becoming too 'trigger happy', and thus helped to reduce tension.

French invasion forces patrol Port Said in Egypt during the Suez War, before the deployment of UNEF I.

Until 1967, both Egypt and Israel saw the advantage of having UNEF on the border (although it was only able to patrol the Egyptian side of the border as the Israelis refused to have UN forces on their territory). In addition, UNEF had the advantage of operating in conditions that were helpful to peacekeeping operations. In the Sinai Desert, it was easy to observe military movements by either side, unhampered by trees, mountains, built-up areas or bad weather conditions.

The Egyptians welcome the UNEF I forces, as they arrive in the Gaza Strip in 1957.

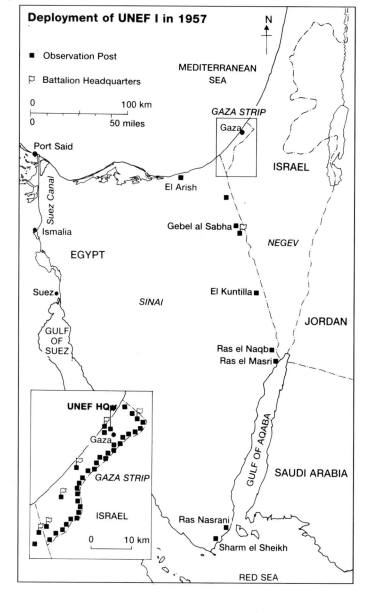

**Deployment of UNEF I in 1957**

N

■ Observation Post

⌐ Battalion Headquarters

0        100 km
0        50 miles

MEDITERRANEAN SEA

*GAZA STRIP*

Gaza

ISRAEL

Port Said

El Arish

Suez Canal

Gebel al Sabha

NEGEV

Ismalia

EGYPT

Suez

El Kuntilla

SINAI

JORDAN

Ras el Naqb
Ras el Masri

UNEF HQ

Gaza

*GAZA STRIP*

ISRAEL

0      10 km

GULF OF SUEZ

GULF OF AQABA

SAUDI ARABIA

Ras Nasrani

Sharm el Sheikh

RED SEA

## The nature of UN peacekeeping

The UN force performed these duties successfully until 1967, when, at the request of the Egyptian government, it was withdrawn. The third Arab–Israeli War, often called the Six-Day War (because that is how long it took for the Israelis to defeat the Arabs) followed. The UN was criticized at the time for removing the UN peacekeeping force, but one of the main characteristics of UN peacekeeping is that the UN can only operate with the agreement of the warring states or the parties to a dispute. This distinguishes UN *peacekeeping* from *peace enforcement*. The idea of UN peacekeeping is built on the belief that the UN should assist in the creation of peace, and it cannot do so without the agreement and support of the parties to a conflict. Once the Egyptian government had withdrawn its consent in 1967, the UN force was obliged to withdraw.

Members of the Yugoslavian contingent of UNEF I observing the Egyptian-Israeli cease-fire line in the Sinai peninsula, near the Gulf of Aqaba.

The need for the consent of the warring parties before the UN peacekeepers can act is not the only feature of UN peacekeeping. UN peacekeepers must keep a neutral position and not take sides with any of the warring parties. Finally, UN peacekeeping forces are generally small compared with the armies involved in the actual conflict, and their policy is to appear as non-threatening as possible.

Troop movements in Sinai during the Six-Day war.

The first UN force in Egypt never went beyond 6,000 troops. Only the large UN peacekeeping forces – those in the Congo (now Zaire) from 1960 to 1964, the forces in the former Yugoslavia during 1992 to 1994 and the UN force in Somalia during 1993 and 1994 – have exceeded 20,000 in number. In addition, UN peacekeeping forces are only lightly armed, and the small observer forces are unarmed, so they do not pose a threat to the parties in a conflict.

**The *Yom Kippur* War**
It was the removal of UNEF in 1967 that led to the Six-Day War. For a number of years, after this conflict came to an end, there was an uneasy peace between Israel and its Arab neighbours. In 1973, however, the Egyptians and the Syrians attacked the Israelis, without warning, on a Jewish holy day, the Day of Atonement, *Yom Kippur*.

Israeli tanks on the move during the *Yom Kippur* War.

**The *Yom Kippur* War**

The 1967 Six-Day War was a disaster for the Arabs. Israel gained much Arab territory, including the Sinai Peninsula and the west bank of the River Jordan.

So, after a number of years rebuilding their arms stocks and with a new leader in the Arab world, President Anwar Sadat of Egypt, the Arabs launched an attack on the Israelis on *Yom Kippur,* in October 1973. For a time, the Arabs looked as though they would win, since the Israelis had to fight a war on two fronts: against the Egyptians and the Syrians. After two weeks of fighting, however, the Israelis had not only driven the Syrians back, but had also crossed deep into Egyptian territory and cut off part of the Egyptian army from retreat. In this situation, the USA and the Soviet Union set up negotiations to end the hostilities. As part of the agreed cease-fire between Israel and the Arabs, two UN peacekeeping forces were established: UNEF II and UNDOF. UNEF II was withdrawn in 1979 after a Peace Treaty was signed between Egypt and Israel. UNDOF is still in position.

## The United Nations Disengagement Observer Force (UNDOF)

The UN was asked to establish peacekeeping forces to separate the Israelis from both the Egyptians and the Syrians. In 1974, UNEF II was set up to operate along the Israeli–Egyptian border, while UNDOF began operating on the Israeli–Syrian border. From its title, it might appear to be an observer force, but it is, in fact, a larger, lightly-armed peacekeeping force. It has successfully performed a number of tasks since it was established.

A Finnish member of UNEF II on observation duty in 1974. This observation post is in the buffer zone between Egyptian and Israeli troops, which was established after the *Yom Kippur* War.

The first task was to ensure that Israel withdrew from most of the Syrian territory that it had captured in the 1973 war. The Israelis pulled their troops back as agreed, and the UN force was put in between the Israelis and the Syrians as a barrier for peace. The Israelis continued to hold the hills, formerly in Syria, called the Golan Heights. These are very important strategically, as they overlook the fertile and prosperous northern part of the small state of Israel.

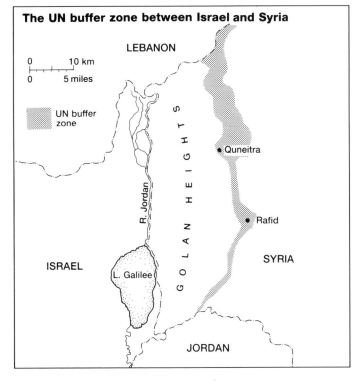

### The UN buffer zone between Israel and Syria

0    10 km

0    5 miles

UN buffer zone

LEBANON

GOLAN HEIGHTS

R. Jordan

• Quneitra

• Rafid

ISRAEL

L. Galilee

SYRIA

JORDAN

The UN Security Council renewing the mandate of UNDOF for six months in November 1975. On this occasion, as the picture shows, the Chinese and Iraqi delegates refused to vote on the resolution.

The Golan Heights were now physically separated from the Syrian army by a buffer zone in which the UN force operated. Both sides have limited the number of weapons and soldiers that are positioned within a distance of 23 km from either side of this zone.

The UN force has performed a second task, in checking on the level of weapons held by Israel and Syria on either side of this zone. In this way, the UN force has been able to reduce the tension between the two states.

A member of UNDOF oversees the cease-fire on the Israel–Syria border in 1973, after the *Yom Kippur* War.

UNDOF has been helped in its tasks by the fact that both Syria and Israel accept the presence of the force operating within the buffer zone. The Israelis have supported UNDOF because its activities have helped to stabilize the border, and in doing so has allowed the Israelis to continue to occupy the Golan Heights, which they consider vital to their security. In this way, the UN presence has 'frozen' the dispute to the advantage of one side. However, the Syrians have shown no desire to overrun the UN positions and disrupt the calm, as they have no wish to start another war with Israel. Moreover, they have a long-running, political dispute with Iraq on their eastern border that occupies much of their attention. In this case, therefore, the UN's role has been broadly supported by either side. UNDOF has been helped by the absence of any other regular or irregular armed groups that could have caused difficulties for the UN in this area of the Middle East. Neither the Israelis nor the Syrians have always allowed UNDOF complete freedom of movement when it is trying to observe the level of weapons in the area on either side of the buffer zone. However, this has not caused too many problems. Like UNEF I and II, UNDOF has been helped by the fact that the landscape and the weather conditions are ideal for the successful performance of its tasks.

**Difficulties faced by the UN in its peacekeeping role**

UNEF I and II and UNDOF were able to operate because, after 1945, the Middle East became the centre of major conflicts in international politics. The superpowers were prepared to allow the UN a role in order to prevent the troubles in the Middle East spreading and threatening their own security. Yet, throughout the Cold War, the superpowers did not allow UN peacekeeping to operate in other areas if it clashed with their interests. The USA did not, for example, allow the UN to intervene in the war in Vietnam, from 1960 to 1975. After invading Hungary in 1956, and Czechoslovakia in 1968, the Soviet Union also stopped the UN from playing any role.

Hungarian citizens fighting against their Soviet-style Communist government in 1956. The Soviet Union sent in troops and tanks to crush the uprising and refused to allow the UN to intervene.

Other factors also stopped the UN from developing its peacekeeping role at this time. The UN needed adequate amounts of money to finance its peacekeeping tasks and a supply of soldiers willing to serve in its forces. Neither of these were immediately available, and, as this book will show, these factors have been crucial to the development of the UN peacekeeping role since 1945.

# PEACEKEEPING – ASSISTING TRANSITION

The division between the superpowers was one of the main factors that restricted the peacekeeping opportunities of the UN during the Cold War. When relations improved between the USA and the Soviet Union in the late 1980s, the two states at last began to co-operate to a much greater extent in the UN. Previously, there had been an atmosphere of suspicion and hostility. This meant that the UN could play a more active role in international politics than it had before and it is now clear that UN peacekeepers are in demand around the world.

The fifth UN Secretary General, Perez de Cuellar, arriving in Angola in August 1983, after visiting South Africa to discuss the UN plan for Namibia. Members of the crowd carry placards supporting the plan, which was carried out in 1989, after the ending of the Cold War.

In the 1980s, the Soviet Union, under President Mikhail Gorbachev, began to pay its share for UN peacekeeping, which it had previously refused to do. The Soviet Union even allowed a small UN force to help the Soviet Army withdraw from Afghanistan from 1988 to 1990. The US government also started to pay off its outstanding debts to the UN and there was, therefore, a more constructive and agreeable atmosphere in the UN Security Council. This was

especially true among the five permanent members of
the council or the P5 – the USA, the Soviet Union
(Russia after 1991), Britain, France and the People's
Republic of China. This co-operation led to the
creation of over twenty UN peacekeeping operations
between 1987 and 1993. These new operations often
gave the UN forces wider responsibilities than before.
In addition, the UN has also felt able to expand the
scope of peacekeeping. For example, some operations
in the 1990s involved the UN using force to try to
achieve its agreed objectives, and not merely to defend
itself. This chapter, together with the next two
chapters, deals with examples of these developments.

## Namibia

South Africa had illegally occupied Namibia since the
Second World War, when it had refused to put the
country under the trusteeship of the UN. A plan for
independence had been drawn up in 1978, but no
progress could be made until the Cold War had ended
and both the Soviet Union and the USA could join
together, with other countries, to put pressure on the
South African government to carry it out.

Perez de Cuellar
inspecting the Kenyan
contingent of UNTAG in
Namibia, in 1989. General
Prem Chand, the force
commander accompanies
him.

FACT FILE

## Namibia

Before the First World War, Namibia (then called South West Africa) was a German colony. After the war, it was administered by South Africa under the League of Nations. After the UN was founded, it wanted to give South West Africa its independence but the South African government refused to allow this. The UN renamed the area Namibia and, in the 1970s, approved a resolution calling for free elections and recognizing the South West African People's Organization (SWAPO) as the true representatives of the Namibian people. In 1978, a settlement plan was created that aimed for Namibian independence, but the South Africans would not leave the area. Part of the reason was that to the north of Namibia, in Angola, there was a civil war taking place in which Soviet-backed Cuban troops were fighting. The South Africans feared that Communism would spread into southern Africa, and thought Namibia would act as a barrier against this. They also felt that if Namibia became independent, Communism might gain a foothold in the territory.

By 1988, the situation in Angola had changed, and the Cold War had ended. South Africa agreed to leave Namibia and the settlement plan was put into operation.

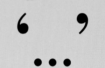

*The UN attaches the highest importance to the Namibian question ... and is determined that the people of the Territory be enabled to exercise their right to self-determination and independence in a free, fair and democratic manner.*

Source: The Secretary General of the UN, Perez de Cuellar, on arriving in South Africa in August 1983, for talks with the government on Namibia

Finnish peacekeepers (above) arrive in Namibia aboard a US Galaxy transport aircraft.

Members of UNTAG (left) carry a wounded SWAPO guerrilla to a helicopter in April 1989.

## The United Nations Transition Assistance Group in Namibia (UNTAG) 1989–90

This force was created in 1989 to help Namibia become independent from South Africa and to carry out the 1978 plan for independence. The UNTAG force had to deal with a range of problems that might prevent Namibia moving peacefully to independence. It was made up of a number of military and civilian sections, each designed to deal with a particular difficulty.

The military sections included a peacekeeping force and an observer unit. The peacekeeping force was made up of three infantry battalions, while the observer unit was made up of 300 military observers, from a number of states. There were also civilian sections made up of election observers, and civilian police, who were there to help to keep law and order.

The military sections had various duties to perform. The first was to make sure that the number of military units operating within Namibia was reduced. This involved checking that the South African Defence Force (SADF), which numbered 30,000 in 1989, was withdrawing as planned. UNTAG also had to ensure that the guerrilla forces of SWAPO, which had fought SADF for independence, were disarmed and encouraged to return to their bases in the adjoining countries of Angola and Zambia. UNTAG wanted there to be no excuse for the SADF to intervene again in Namibia.

Members of the British contingent to UNTAG on patrol in Namibia in 1989.

The second task was to keep Namibia free from any outside interference, while it moved to independence. UNTAG military units were posted along Namibia's borders to make sure that groups of people that might want to cause trouble were not allowed to enter the country.

However, at the very beginning, UNTAG personnel were very thin on the ground. When SWAPO guerrillas crossed over the border from Angola into Namibia, threatening the holding of free elections, UNTAG was not strong enough to hold them back. As a part solution, the UN allowed the SADF to stop the SWAPO advance. However, this was a dangerous course of action, because UNTAG's neutral position could have been brought in to question. A new cease-fire was only agreed after much diplomatic activity, which went on for many weeks, and the SWAPO guerrillas were persuaded to return to their bases. This dangerous situation had happened because of attempts to save money on the use of UNTAG forces, and SWAPO had intervened at a time when the force was weak. UNTAG then had to make sure that the new cease-fire between SWAPO and the SADF held, in order to provide stable and peaceful conditions for the elections.

SWAPO troops killed by the SADF, in the border areas of Namibia, in September 1989. The South Africans continued to operate in Namibia until October 1989.

Elections in Namibia were held under UN supervision. Here are some of the electoral monitors at work.

The civilian section of UNTAG was made up of a group of electoral monitors and a large, civilian police force. The electoral monitors were there, first to establish procedures for the elections, and then to explain to the Namibians, who had never voted before, how they would be carried out. During the elections in November 1989, the monitors were present to make sure that they were held in a correct fashion – free, fair and without corruption, and that the voters were not intimidated or threatened.

The civilian police were made part of UNTAG to assist in the maintenance of law and order, and to monitor the activities of the South West African Police (SWAPOL) which was controlled by South Africa. People were afraid that SWAPOL would try to undermine the elections, therefore, UNTAG's police were increased from 500 to 1,500 by October 1989. They were often viewed with hostility by the local police, but they were able to ensure the registration of about 700,000 voters for the elections. Of these, more than 90 per cent actually voted.

UNTAG's operations in Namibia were highly successful, and it was the first peacekeeping operation of its kind that was given the responsibility for assisting a state to become independent. The civilian sections of UNTAG were essential to the success of the UN operation, as was the fact that it had political support from a number of states, all of which hoped it would succeed.

## Cambodia

The success of UNTAG in Namibia, in preparing a country for independence, was a factor in encouraging the UN to send a peacekeeping force to Cambodia.

SWAPO supporters await the election results in Namibia.

**FACT FILE**

**Civil war in Cambodia**
At the end of the
Vietnam War in 1975,
Vietnam's neighbour,
Cambodia, came under
the control of the
Communist Khmer
Rouge army, led by Pol
Pot. He began a reign of
terror in Cambodia
(renamed Kampuchea)
in which over one million
people were killed. In
1979, Vietnam,
supported by the Soviet
Union, invaded
Cambodia and drove the
Khmer Rouge out.
Throughout the 1980s
there was a civil war in
Cambodia as guerrilla
groups fought the
Vietnam-backed
Cambodian government.
By the end of the 1980s,
it was clear that there
would be no clear winner
in this situation.

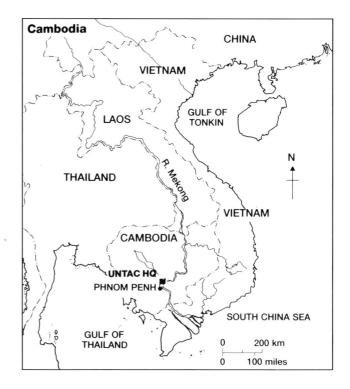

### The United Nations Transitional Authority in Cambodia (UNTAC)

In 1989, the various groups that had been fighting
for control in Cambodia agreed to allow the UN to
observe elections to choose a new government.
UNTAC, a mixed force of 22,000 military, police
and civilian personnel, was sent to Cambodia in
March 1992. It had many different tasks and the
operation was the most ambitious peacekeeping
enterprise the UN had ever undertaken. UNTAC's
duties included overseeing the cease-fire among

the four warring groups and disarming them, clearing mines, providing election monitors to oversee the elections for a new Cambodian government, held in April and May 1993, and supplying civilian workers to administer many areas of government in the run-up to the election. In this programme, UN peacekeepers took on new roles. UN peacekeepers had not, before this, become involved in the government of a country to which they had been sent. In Cambodia, for a brief while before the elections, the UN force was the government.

Cambodian refugees returning from Thailand in 1992 to vote under UN protection.

Members of the Khmer People's National Liberation Armed Forces (left) waiting to be disarmed by the UN force in Cambodia, 1992.

By 1994, most of the UNTAC personnel had left the country, and the new Cambodian government was in place. A guerrilla campaign was still being fought in parts of the country by the forces of the Khmer Rouge, but Cambodia was in a far more stable and peaceful condition than it had been before UNTAC arrived.

# PEACEKEEPING – MODERATING CIVIL WARS

**The UN in former Yugoslavia**

The previous chapter showed an example of successful internal peacekeeping, by UN forces, while helping Namibia to gain independence. The focus of this chapter will again be on internal peacekeeping, where the UN has been involved in trying to calm a civil war in some areas of the country which was formerly Yugoslavia.

Yugoslavia, with its unstable mixture of different nationalities, religions, languages and traditions, became a Communist country under the strong leadership of Marshal Tito after the Second World War. Tito died in 1980. By 1989, however, Communism was in decline across the whole of Eastern Europe, including the Soviet Union. Once the old Communist Party had lost its power in Yugoslavia, cultural and religious differences and the old, bitter rivalries came to the surface. The country began to break up into smaller, separate states.

**' '**
**• • •**

*'May God protect you the way you protected us.'*

Source: A placard, at a protest by Bosnians against the visit of the UN Secretary General, Boutros Boutros-Ghali, to Sarajevo, in January 1993

*'How many more victims are needed for you to do something? Would a million be enough for you Mr Ghali? Would you do something then or would you let us defend ourselves?'*

Source: Vedrana Bozinovic, a reporter for Studio 99, a television station in Sarajevo, in January 1993

*'Forget negotiations, we should just go in and hammer them.'*

Source: A French sergeant major in UNPROFOR, sick of being the target of snipers' bullets in Bosnia, January 1993

The body of a woman lying in the street, the victim of a sniper's bullet in Sarajevo, the capital of Bosnia, in 1992.

## The provinces of Yugoslavia

KEY

 Serbs

Croats

Macedonians

Montenegrins

Slovenes

Moslems

0    100 km

0    50 miles

HUNGARY

N

SLOVENIA
Ljubljana
Zagreb
CROATIA

ROMANIA

VOJVODINA
Novi Sad
Belgrade

BOSNIA
HERCEGOVINA
Sarajevo

SERBIA

ADRIATIC
SEA

MONTENEGRO   Pristina

BULGARIA

Titograd   KOSOVO

ITALY

Skopje

MACEDONIA

ALBANIA

GREECE

---

FACT FILE

### Yugoslavia

Yugoslavia became an independent state at the end of the First World War. It was formed from territories that were once part of the Empire of Austria–Hungary and from the Kingdom of Serbia and Bosnia–Hercegovina, two states that had previously belonged to the Turkish Empire.

From the start, Yugoslavia was not a unified state. It was made up of six regions: Serbia, Croatia, Slovenia, Bosnia, Macedonia and Montenegro. Within these regions, there were distinct national areas such as Serbia, but Serbs were also to be found living in parts of Croatia and Bosnia. Yugoslavia was also divided by religion: the Croats and Slovenes were mainly Roman Catholic, while the Serbs were Serbian Orthodox, and the Bosnians were Muslim.

A UN plane lands at Sarajevo airport as a UN convoy awaits the Bosnian Serbs' permission to allow aid to be delivered to the besieged town of Gorazde, 1994.

**The United Nations Protection Force (UNPROFOR)**

UNPROFOR was sent to Croatia in 1992, after a war had broken out between Serbia and Croatia. It was designed to separate those Serbs who had always lived in some parts of Croatia from the Croats after the war had ended. Its role was to promote calm and increase confidence between the two warring states.

In 1993, another part of the force was sent to Macedonia, in the south, to discourage any ethnic conflict spreading from Serbia into Macedonia. If this had happened, all the Balkans could have been dragged into a war that would involve Greece, Albania and Bulgaria, as well as former Yugoslavia. This second part of the force was engaged in what the UN Secretary General, Boutros-Ghali, called 'preventive deployment': the aim being to discourage rival groups and armed bands from fighting, by the presence of UN forces.

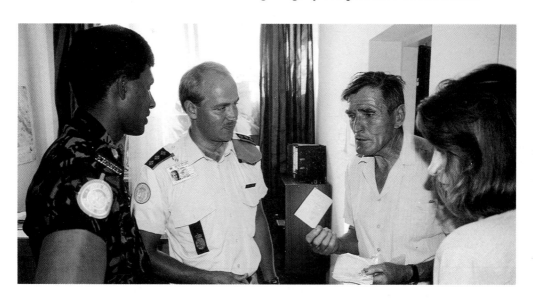

A Croatian villager trying to contact relatives in the town of Split asks for help from the UN civilian police as part of UNPROFOR, 1992.

A third part of the UN force operating in Bosnia was the one that gained the most attention and experienced the most difficulties. In early 1992, after Bosnia declared itself independent, a civil war broke out involving Bosnian Serbs, Bosnian Croats and the Bosnian Muslims. The Serbs and Croats were hoping to expand the areas under their control by defeating the Bosnian Muslims, and thus dividing most of Bosnia between themselves.

Many towns and cities, populated mainly by Muslims, were surrounded by armed Bosnian Serbs, determined to bring about the surrender of the Muslims and then move them by force to other parts of Bosnia. This practice became known as 'ethnic cleansing'. Croat forces attacked other Muslim areas, and Muslim troops tried to capture areas populated by Croats. During this bitter civil war, everyday life in Bosnia broke down: towns were shelled, army snipers killed civilians in the streets, airports were shut down and roads were closed. Large sections of the Bosnian population were held hostage in the towns, unable to escape, or to live a normal life. It was very difficult for people to find food and medical supplies began to run out.

A member of the Danish contingent to UNPROFOR on observation duties with the force in Croatia in 1992.

Part of the British contingent of UNPROFOR leads a UNHCR relief convoy with 40 tonnes of food through Bosnia, November 1992.

Faced with this situation, the UN High Commission for Refugees (UNHCR) and a number of international aid agencies organized relief supplies of food and essential materials to be sent to the besieged Bosnian people. It was often dangerous to deliver these essential goods to the trapped Bosnian Muslims. In order to reach their destinations, convoys of lorries had to drive from the coast on bad, mountainous roads, that were patrolled by Serbian and Croatian troops. Often these patrols were hostile and obstructive. Without protection, the relief supplies could not get through to the starving and desperate people who needed them. So, eventually, UNPROFOR was given the responsibility of protecting these supply convoys.

### The role of UNPROFOR in Bosnia

The Bosnian Muslims hoped UNPROFOR would be able to lift the siege of many of the towns and prevent the destruction of their country. However, they were soon to be disappointed, and dissatisfaction with the UN force spread quickly. UNPROFOR could not use force to protect them, as it was not permitted to do this by the UN Security Council, or by the governments who had contributed troops to the operation.

UNPROFOR's role was limited to escorting the aid convoys. Since it was a peacekeeping force, it could only use military force in self-defence. The use of road blocks by Serbs and Croats to delay the delivery of aid caused the major problem and UNPROFOR had no solution to this. In the beginning, it had no authority to use force to push the shipments of aid through, or to dismantle the road blocks. It could only negotiate with the Serbs and Croats, where possible, for the removal of obstructions to allow the aid through. If that was not possible, the essential food and medical supplies remained stranded on roads in Bosnia. This frustrating situation was made worse by the fact that the powerlessness of the UN was captured regularly on television cameras and transmitted across the world. It was not surprising, therefore, that the UN Secretary General, Boutros-Ghali was met by hostile Muslims when he visited Sarajevo in 1993.

Members of the French contingent of UNPROFOR inspect Lovinac, a village destroyed by Bosnian Serbs.

In an attempt to do something more positive for the Muslims, the UN Security Council passed a resolution in 1993 that permitted the UN to use force in order to get aid through. It also created a number of safe havens in besieged towns and surrounding areas, in order to prevent them from being attacked. In addition, the UN threatened the Serbs with air-strikes if they continued the shelling of towns. This resolution did not, however, assist the UN troops on the ground. Although they then had the legal right to use force, they did not have the necessary military resources to get involved in a shooting war with the Serb or Croat armies. The number of UNPROFOR troops in Bosnia, in 1994, was only 22,000. The UN found it difficult to find more troops to serve in Bosnia, and those states that had provided troops were reluctant to approve air-strikes or other military action, as they feared reprisals against their own troops by the Serbs.

UN troops patrolling Sarajevo airport in 1992. The airport was later to be closed by Serbs who prevented supplies from reaching Sarajevo, in order to try to starve out the Bosnian Muslims.

FEDERATION     UNITED KINGDOM     UNITED STAT

The Security Council discusses the imposition of sanctions against Serbia and Montenegro, in 1992, to try to stop them supporting the Bosnian Serbs.

**Serbs hold up British convoy for fourth day**

Serb forces continued for a fourth day … to hold up a convoy of 168 British troops bound for Gorazde in spite of the UN/Nato air-strike ultimatum and an agreement with the UN.

The company-sized unit from the Duke of Wellington's Regiment has been prevented by the Serbs from entering the town since last Friday. As soon as one obstruction was surmounted, the Serbs replaced it with another…

Under the UN/Nato ultimatum of April 22, Serb forces risk air-strikes if they do not withdraw their troops to at least three kilometres from the town centre and pull back their heavy weapons to more than twenty kilometres. A second condition is that UN personnel are to have free and unhindered access to the enclave.

Source: *The Times*, June 1994

**Terror and mayhem in Gorazde 'Life is measured in seconds not years'**

Serbian shells rained down on the crammed and cowering inhabitants of Gorazde yesterday, as aid workers in the towns and UN officials predicted an imminent catastrophe.

*'Shells are dropping at random on the town centre,'* said a report from the four staff of the UN High Commissioner for Refugees in the town. *'The hospital has taken a direct hit on the roof. The Red Cross refugee centre has been hit. At least five shells fell in front of the hospital. Impacts are continuing every twenty seconds.'*

Source: *Guardian*, April 1994

UN soldiers inspect the site where a British-led UN convoy was attacked by Bosnian Serbs, near Sarajevo, in July 1994.

The Bosnian Muslims felt that the UN was trying to keep them alive through aid deliveries only to allow them to be killed by Serb shells, or to be ethnically cleansed. Some believed that the UN was taking the side of the Serbs and Croats against them. However, the Serbs also accused the UN force of taking sides, and charged the UN with delivering arms and weapons to the Muslims in the food convoys. The UN had imposed an arms embargo to try to stop weapon supplies to all the warring groups. The situation worked mostly against the Muslims in that the Serbs were able to use the military equipment of the former Yugoslav army, as well as receive arms from parts of eastern Europe. The Croats were able to get a supply of arms from parts of western Europe, leaving the Bosnian Muslims in a weak position.

By 1994, it was expected that UNPROFOR might have to withdraw from Bosnia. There seemed to be no peace settlement acceptable to all parties, and morale in the force was low. While the UN had the authority to use force, there was no political will among member states to turn it into action. This led to disagreements between the UN Secretary General and the military commanders on the ground, some of whom wanted to use force against the Serbs. This was changed in February 1994, when the Serbs had shelled a food queue in Sarajevo and killed over seventy civilians. The Serbs were told to remove their heavy guns and tanks from the area around Sarajevo or risk air-strikes by NATO planes against them. These strikes would be

UN troops move a Bosnian Serb gun, 1994. This followed a UN/NATO ultimatum, requiring that the Serbs should remove heavy weapons from around Sarajevo.

carried out in support of the 1993 UN resolution. This first ultimatum had the desired effect but it, and others which followed, did little to force agreement to a peace settlement. In 1994, an international plan was drawn up to end the war, but the Bosnian Serbs refused to accept it. In November 1994, NATO air forces, in support of the UN, bombed Serb positions around the safe haven of Bihac in Bosnia after it had come under attack by Bosnian Serb forces. The former US President Carter then negotiated a cease-fire among the parties in Bosnia, but many people doubted that this would hold as many previous ones had been broken.

In response to all these difficulties, there were two broad views. The first was that the UN should leave Bosnia as its presence was only delaying the inevitable. Serbs, Croats and Bosnians would have to reach a settlement by themselves, and the intervention of the UN force was actually preventing this from happening. The other view was that, if the UN did withdraw, the war could spread to other parts of former Yugoslavia such as Macedonia, and there could be the risk of a widespread Balkan war.

The experience of UNPROFOR shows the frustrations and difficulties that arise when a peacekeeping force is put into a situation such as a complex civil war, without the necessary political and military support. If the UN were to try to enforce peace in Bosnia and go beyond the peacekeeping role, it would require a

**Bosnia in November 1994**

↑N

SLOVENIA

HUNGARY

● Zagreb

CROATIA

More than 1,000 Bangladeshi
UN peacekeepers in
Bihac enclave ──── Bosnian Serb attacks

VOJVODINA

●Erdut

●Orasje

● Bihac

Banja Luka ●

BOSNIA HERCEGOVINA

Ubdina ●

Tuzla ●

Belgrade
●

54 Canadian UN
peacekeepers detained
at Visoko by
Bosnian Serbs

SERBIA

Travnik ●

● Zadar

● Vitez

Visoko

● Srebrenica

G Vakuf ●

●

SARAJEVO

250 French, Ukrainian
and Canadian
peacekeepers
held hostage
around Sarajevo

● Split

●Gorazde

Mostar ●

MONTENEGRO

Muslims in Bosnia and Croatia

Serbs in Bosnia and Croatia

0                    100 km

0              50 miles

ADRIATIC SEA

ALBANIA

commitment by states to provide an army of over
100,000 troops, possibly for a long period of time, and
certainly for years rather than months. In 1994, there
was not much evidence that member states of the UN
were prepared to provide this, because of the political,
financial and military costs involved. Some member
states, particularly Russia, were uneasy about the UN
authorizing air-strikes against the Serbs. In the next
chapter we shall see what can happen when the UN
does use force, as in Somalia.

### Serbs set to sweep into Bihac

Eyewitness reports described the Serbs advancing to within one and a half miles of the city centre 'like a medieval army' destroying houses and villages in their wake. The fighting continued long after nightfall.

In Sarajevo, Lt Gen. Sir Michael Rose, the UN commander in Bosnia, said last night that it would be 'tragic' if the Serbs carried out their threat to occupy the besieged city.

But he admitted: *'There is a limit to how much force we can use in a peacekeeping mission. We should only use force when there is direct targeting of the civilian population or my own troops in the Bihac pocket.'*

Source: *Daily Telegraph*, November 1994

### UK voters want troops to stay

A large majority of voters is opposed to withdrawing United Nations troops from Bosnia, according to a ... poll for the *Guardian*. The issue is being considered by a Cabinet committee today.

Only 23 per cent of the voters support an immediate pullout of UN troops, while a total of 67 per cent support three other options which would leave the 23,000 UN servicemen in Bosnia...

The poll suggests that the risk of British servicemen losing their lives has made little impact on public opinion.

That could change rapidly if more British troops came under fire or were taken hostage, as has happened to Bangladeshi and Canadian UN forces.

In view of the renewed fighting in Bosnia should UN troops be:

|  | NOW | Men | Women | 18–24 | 65+ | 1993 poll |
|---|---|---|---|---|---|---|
| Pulled out immediately | 23 | 29 | 18 | 20 | 38 | 20 |
| Kept in current humanitarian role | 22 | 21 | 24 | 18 | 18 | 22 |
| Kept in hope a peace plan emerges | 22 | 18 | 25 | 25 | 20 | 40 |
| Upgraded to a combat role | 23 | 26 | 20 | 27 | 15 | 9 |
| Don't know | 10 | 7 | 13 | 9 | 10 | 9 |

Source: *Guardian*, December 1994

[The figures show the views of different groups of people in percentages.]

# PEACEKEEPING – CONTROLLING CIVIL WARS

## Somalia

Somalia, in the Horn of Africa, became a focus of international concern after 1991, when the government of President Siad Barre was overthrown. This left the country very unstable. Widespread fighting broke out among different groups, headed by warlords, each struggling to take control of the state. This turned into civil war, and the country gradually descended into chaos. This disorder was accompanied by large-scale famine across the country. By the beginning of 1992, the situation in Somalia was desperate. Relief supplies in the form of food and medical necessities, organized by international charities, were only able to get through to their destinations with the agreement and co-operation of the local warlords who controlled different parts of the country. Many people fled across the borders as refugees.

A starving family in Somalia that has fortunately managed to reach a feeding centre, 1992. Many people died of hunger because widespread disorder throughout the country disrupted the distribution of food supplies.

**FACT FILE**

**Somalia**

Somalia is strategically important as it overlooks the sea routes between the Red Sea and the Indian Ocean. During the Cold War, both the USA and the Soviet Union made use of the naval bases in Somalia and also sold weapons to the Somali government. As a result of this, Somalia had a lot of weapons which got into the hands of tribal gangs. In 1991, the Somali dictator, Siad Barre, was overthrown by a rival, and civil war broke out between the different tribes under local warlords.

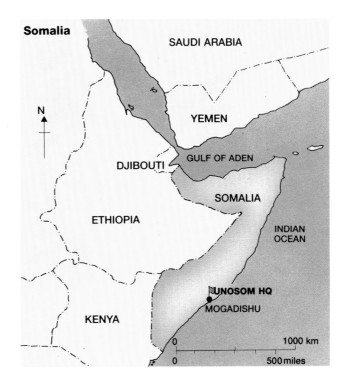

Somalia

Organized gangs loot relief supplies at one of Somalia's ports, 1992.

The UN decided to act to assist the distribution of the relief supplies. Acting under Chapter VII of the UN Charter, the Security Council passed a resolution in January 1992 imposing an arms embargo on Somalia. This was intended to stop the different factions in the civil war obtaining further military supplies. In March of the same year, a cease-fire was arranged by the UN in Mogadishu, the capital of Somalia. The Secretary General then proposed that a small observer force should be created to monitor the cease-fire. He also proposed that a 500-strong peacekeeping force should be assembled, to escort the relief supplies from Somalia's ports to distribution centres throughout the country.

In December 1992, the Security Council votes unanimously to set up the unified Task Force (UNITAF) under US command. Its purpose was to make it possible to distribute food supplies more efficiently in Somalia.

## United Nations Operation in Somalia (UNOSOM)

The peacekeeping force, UNOSOM I, was organized on traditional lines. It therefore had, in theory, to act with the agreement of the government of the country in which it found itself. In Somalia, however, there was no host government, but a number of groups, all claiming to have authority. In this situation, the UN had to win the agreement of the main warring groups to the formation of the force. This took time, and therefore the main part of UNOSOM I did not begin to operate until September and October 1992. Following the arrival of the Pakistani troops in UNOSOM I, another resolution was passed that was intended to expand the numbers in the force. It was hoped that this would allow it to extend its peacekeeping and escort functions over the whole of Somalia.

Unfortunately, the UN force was never able to fulfil its tasks. The Pakistani troops in UNOSOM I were attacked by the warring factions, and found it impossible either to protect the delivery of the relief supplies, or to secure the cease-fire. Since other

Installing radio equipment into a jeep belonging to the Pakistani contingent to UNOSOM I, 1992. Communications were to be a major problem for the UN forces in Somalia.

countries were not willing to commit troops to Somalia, the force was never expanded. The civil war dragged on and many Somalis continued to die of starvation.

**Operation Restore Hope**

The US government, therefore, proposed the creation of a task force, under the command of the USA, not the UN, to go into Somalia. Its purpose would be to make sure that food and medical supplies were distributed, using force if necessary. The UN Security Council agreed to the setting up of this force in December 1992, and the first US troops were sent into Somalia under Operation Restore Hope.

As many as twenty-nine states joined the coalition, under US command, in the Unified Task Force (UNITAF). There were then two forces operating in Somalia: the small UNOSOM I, which was governed by traditional peacekeeping rules, and therefore could only use force in self-defence, and UNITAF, which could use force to protect the delivery of the relief supplies. The US government, however, did not wish to see UNITAF remain in Somalia: the objective of the force was to deliver the relief supplies, feed the starving people of Somalia, and then withdraw.

## UNOSOM II

Once UNITAF had achieved a level of stability, and relief supplies began to reach their targets, the UN assumed responsibility for security in Somalia with the creation of a new UN force in May 1993. It was expected that this force, UNOSOM II, could be made up of as many as 28,000 personnel, although it never reached that number. It was unusual in that Resolution 813 allowed it to use force from the beginning, in order to achieve its objectives of maintaining peace, disarming warring factions, and protecting relief operations. It was expected that UNOSOM II would cover the whole of Somalia and eventually help in rebuilding the country. The USA had expected to leave Somalia once UNITAF had handed over its responsibility to UNOSOM II, but it found that many states welcomed the US support for UNOSOM II. Therefore, 4,000 US troops remained under UN command to support UNOSOM II's operations. Rather confusingly, a separate US unit, a rapid reaction force, remained, but was not under UN command.

An Arab member of UNITAF guards Somalis near a food distribution centre in Mogadishu, 1993.

US forces on patrol in Somalia in 1993.

**UN moves to crack down on Somali warlords**
**The Mogadishu rebels have joined the Bosnian Serbs, the Khmer Rouge and Unita in defying world peacekeepers. This time Boutros-Ghali has pledged to act.**

The weekend insurrection in Somalia which prompted the UN Security Council to pass a resolution last night calling for the arrest, prosecution and trial of those who killed [twenty-four] Pakistani peacekeepers in Somalia, was the worst attack on the organization's forces since the ill-fated intervention in the Congo in 1961, when forty-four Ghanaian 'blue berets' were massacred.

The shootout in Mogadishu on Saturday, which also left twenty-three Somalis dead after other UN peacekeepers unearthed a large weapons cache, pushed Boutros-Ghali, the UN Secretary General, into calling for 'prompt and firm action against the perpetrators of this crime...'

The death toll in Mogadishu delivers a clear warning of things to come from Somali warlords who have found that their power bases are being eroded by foreign troops in the country.

The fighting in Mogadishu was apparently provoked by an attempt by ... Pakistani peacekeepers to inspect a weapons depot controlled by forces loyal to General Aidid. Mogadishu was rocked by the sounds of grenades, automatic weapons and heavy machine-gun fire from helicopters, as what had been a routine inspection of an armoury belonging to the city's strongest militia, developed into street fighting.

Source: *The Times,* June 1993

The problems of UNOSOM II and the remaining US troops were highlighted in June 1993, when twenty-four Pakistani troops from UNOSOM II were killed in an ambush by Somalis, probably those under the leadership of General Aidid, the strongest warlord in Somalia. General Aidid and his supporters had denounced the UN intervention as interference in the

Members of UNOSOM II on duty in Somalia in 1993.

internal affairs of the country, and warned the UN to confine itself to relief work. This attitude underlined the difficulties the UN was facing in Somalia. The peace in the country could not be guaranteed unless the warring groups could be disarmed and the leaders rounded up. The UN tried to do this unsuccessfully throughout 1993. The UN and the US troops, under separate command, resorted to heavy attacks against the warring groups including the use of helicopter gunships. Many of these attacks were ineffective since the UN force, and the US troops, who had remained in Somalia, were unable to pinpoint the position of these groups accurately. They often attacked the wrong targets and killed innocent civilians. In September, 200 people, mostly women and children were killed when a US combat helicopter fired on a crowd. These incidents created a very bad image for the UN, and led to tension within UNOSOM II, as some of the contributing countries, particularly Italy, criticized the way in which operations were being carried out. The situation reached a head in October 1993, when, in an attempt to capture supporters of General Aidid, eighteen US troops were killed and over seventy injured. The US government, under President Clinton, stated that it intended to withdraw all US troops from Somalia. This prompted other states to announce their intention to leave UNOSOM II.

**Problems highlighted by UN action in Somalia**
The experience of UNOSOM II showed that any decision to use force by the UN needs careful consideration.

Because UNOSOM II was given the right to use force from the start in order to achieve its objectives, it was not always clear when it was acting as a peacekeeping force and when it was acting as a coercive force. It therefore lost the support of many of the Somalis whom it was trying to help.

Somali women express their views on UN action in Somalia – note the signs are written in English.

Many of the troops in UNOSOM II were neither well-trained nor experienced. There was a breakdown in communications in the country between many of the units, and there were problems over command and control of the force. The UN was shown to lack the information and intelligence that it needed in order to identify the many warring groups and their locations. Consequently, small but well-armed groups were able to inflict unacceptable damage on a UN force that was not trained for confrontation.

Because of problems such as these, UN casualties in enforcement operations are always likely to be greater than those in peacekeeping operations. Governments must expect this to be the case if they provide troops for future UN operations that move from peacekeeping to enforcement in the course of the operation.

# CONCLUSION

The UN's record as a peacekeeper since 1945 has been a mixed one and it has faced many problems in trying to keep the peace.

First of all, in any situation, there needs to be some peace to keep. If the actions of the UN are not supported by those involved in the dispute, there is very little that a UN peacekeeping force can do.

One of the most important reasons why some of the UN peacekeeping operations have failed has been the attitude of the major powers in the Security Council. During the Cold War, the superpowers were reluctant to allow the UN to operate in areas under their influence. Since the ending of the Cold War, the UN has intervened in many parts of the globe, but often without the political, financial and military support necessary to achieve its peacekeeping goals. These are all vital to the success of a UN operation.

Political support from member states is essential if a UN force is to be set up and operate successfully. In addition, a UN force needs a clear mandate and instructions on what it is expected to do and achieve. It must also have the long-term support of the major powers, once in the field of operations, to back it up if it is prevented from carrying out its tasks.

Throughout the 1990s, although the international community has felt that 'something must be done' in response to wars across the world, it has not always been prepared to give full support to UN forces in the field of operations.

For many years, the former Soviet Union would not pay for UN peacekeeping and, in the 1980s, the USA began to fall behind in its contributions to the UN budget. Although the end of the Cold War changed the attitude of the superpowers to paying

Dr Boutros-Ghali, the sixth UN Secretary General, on a visit to Somalia in 1993.

**FACT FILE**

**How peacekeeping is funded**
The UN is financed by assessed and by voluntary contributions from member states. Assessed contributions cover the UN budget and the special peacekeeping accounts set up to support each peacekeeping force. The amount each state contributes to the UN budget is linked to its national income, while the amount it pays to the peacekeeping accounts are in proportion to the amount it has to pay to the regular budget. The economically powerful states are assessed by the UN at a higher rate than the developing states and thus pay more.
The Cyprus force (UNFICYP) has from the start been financed by voluntary contributions.

for the UN, there is still a large shortfall on the UN peacekeeping budget. This has become larger as the number of UN peacekeeping forces has increased. By the middle of 1994, there were over 70,000 troops, and civilian police from seventy countries serving with UN peacekeeping forces across the world. The cost of these operations was US $3.2 billion per year, yet over one third of these annual costs had not been paid by member states. By October 1994, the USA owed US $453 million and Russia US $569 million.

The US government was reluctant to see the UN incur further debts through the creation of more peacekeeping forces, and states are now reluctant to provide military and civilian police forces for peacekeeping operations as they fear they will not be paid by the UN for their contributions.

Governments are also concerned that their troops will be placed in great danger in some of these operations. This has been particularly true of the UN forces in Bosnia and Somalia, where the UN has operated in the middle of civil wars.

Members of the Irish contingent to UNFICYP (right) at a signal post in Famagusta, Cyprus, in 1964.

**The United Nations force in Cyprus (UNFICYP)**

UNFICYP is an interesting example of a UN peacekeeping force that began as an internal force but, following a change in circumstances, successfully changed into a border patrol force.

In 1960, the island of Cyprus gained independence from Britain. The island was mostly Greek, but had a large Turkish minority (18 per cent of the population). By 1964, the government of the island had broken down as a result of Greek–Cypriot and Turkish–Cypriot rivalries. Fighting broke out between the two communities and there was a danger that Greece and Turkey would go to war over the island. In order to prevent this, the UN sent a force of peacekeepers to Cyprus in March 1964, to monitor a cease-fire, to assist in the restoration of law and order and to keep the peace.

Although there were periodic outbursts of fighting, the UN force performed well until 1974. In that year, the Turks, provoked by a movement to unite the island with the rest of Greece, invaded Cyprus. Since then, the island has been divided into two parts and UNFICYP has patrolled the border between the Turkish Republic of Northern Cyprus and the remainder of the island.

## The Future

'To remain calm in the face of provocation, to maintain composure when under attack, the United Nations troops, officers and soldiers alike, must show a special kind of courage, one that is more difficult to come by than the ordinary kind. Our United Nations troops have been put to the test and have emerged triumphant.'

Source: Javier Perez de Cuellar, UN Secretary General 1982–91

Following the end of the Cold War, many people became optimistic about what the UN might be able to do in the future. Some of this optimism has been lost, as the UN has been seen to fail in its aims in Bosnia and Somalia. Yet, the UN can only be as efficient and as strong as its member states wish it to be.

There are some improvements that could be made in the organization of the UN that would assist it in its peacekeeping role. This includes providing better military intelligence for the Secretary General. Member states could also identify and select troops, within their own armed forces, to be available for UN duty should the UN require them. Until the international community reaches agreement about what the role of the UN should be, and is prepared to support that role, UN peacekeeping will remain a valuable but limited service to world peace.

The value of the UN's work is recognized. The UN Secretary General, Perez de Cuellar, receives the Nobel Peace Prize in Oslo, Norway in 1988, on behalf of UN peacekeeping forces.

NOBEL PEACE PRIZE 1988

UNITED NATIONS PEACE-KEEPING

# GLOSSARY

**Axis Powers** The coalition of Germany, Italy and Japan, which fought the Allies (Britain and the Commonwealth and, from 1941, the USA, Russia and China) in the Second World War.

**Balkans** The area of south-eastern Europe consisting of the former Yugoslavia, Bulgaria, Greece, Albania, part of Romania and European Turkey.

**bloc** A group of states which have the same political or military interests.

**coalition** A group of states which ally with each other to achieve a particular goal.

**Cold War** The name used to describe the bad relations between the USA and the Soviet Union and their respective allies from 1946–89.

**Czechoslovakian Revolution** A revolution that occurred in 1968, when the Communist Party in Czechoslovakia tried to reform the political system. The Soviet Union saw this as a threat to Communism, so troops from the Warsaw Pact countries were sent to overthrow the new government.

**ethnic conflict** Fighting between groups because of national, religious or cultural differences.

**ethnic cleansing** The forced removal of a particular group of people from an area, because of their national, religious or cultural identity.

**Hungarian Uprising** A popular uprising in Hungary, in 1956, against Communism, which was brutally put down by the Soviet army.

**The League of Nations** An international organization, with the aim of achieving world peace, which was set up in 1919, after the First World War. The USA was not a member. It was replaced by the UN.

**mandate** The set of tasks that the UN gives to a peacekeeping or observer force and the rules within which it must work.

**Nationalist China** China from 1928–49 when it was ruled by a Nationalist government. This government was overthrown by the Communists, led by Mao Zedong, in 1949. The Nationalists retreated to the island of Taiwan and set up government there.

**North Atlantic Treaty Organization** An alliance of 16 states, including the USA, created in 1949 to defend Europe against any military threat from the Soviet bloc.

**observer forces** UN forces who have a limited role, normally the monitoring and reporting of incidents. These forces are generally small in number and carry limited arms. Peacekeeping forces are larger, have wider responsibilities and are better armed, but can still only use force in self-defence.

**People's Republic of China** The government which was set up in 1949 by the Chinese Communist Party (see Nationalist China).

**preventive deployment** The policy put forward by UN Secretary General, Boutros-Ghali, of involving the UN in disputes at an early stage before they become too big to resolve easily.

**resolution** A statement of intentions put forward by the UN General Assembly and the Security Council which is then voted on by member states.

**Second World War** A world war fought from 1939–45 between the Allies and Germany, Italy and Japan (see Axis Powers).

**trusteeship** The authority given to a state to look after the well-being of another state or territory.

**ultimatum** A final demand from one or more states to another state or states that, if not agreed to, will lead to some further action, such as war.

**UN High Commission for Refugees** An office of the UN General Assembly that seeks to monitor and assist refugees who have fled from their homeland.

**UN Secretary General** The chief administrator of the UN who often has to act like a political leader, but is neither a head of government nor a head of state.

**Vietnam War** A war fought by the USA and the Republic of South Vietnam from 1964–75 against North Vietnam and the Vietcong Communist organization.

**Warsaw Pact** An alliance of seven Communist states in Europe – the Soviet Union, East Germany, Poland, Czechoslovakia, Hungary, Romania, Bulgaria – which existed during the Cold War period.

# BOOKS TO READ

Buckley, Richard (ed.) *The United Nations: Overseeing the New World Order* (European Schoolbooks Publishing Ltd, 1993)

King, John *Conflict in the Middle East* (Wayland, 1993)

Flint, David *Bosnia* (Franklin Watts, 1994)

Ross, Stewart *United Nations* (Wayland, 1993)

## UNITED NATIONS PEACEKEEPING AND OBSERVER FORCES SINCE 1945

in chronological order

**Forces created during the Cold War**
UNTSO United Nations Truce Supervision Organization
UNMOGIP United Nations Military Observer Group in India and Pakistan
UNEF I United Nations Emergency Force I
UNOGIL United Nations Observer Group in Lebanon
ONUC UN Operation in the Congo.
UNSF United Nations Security Force
UNYOM United Nations Yemen Observer Mission
UNFICYP United Nations Force in Cyprus
UNIPOM United Nations India–Pakistan Observer Mission
UNEF II United Nations Emergency Force II
UNDOF United Nations Disengagement Observer Force
UNIFIL United Nations Interim Force in Lebanon

**Forces created since the end of the Cold War**
UNGOMAP United Nations Good Offices Mission to Afghanistan and Pakistan
UNIIMOG United Nations Iran–Iraq Military Observer Group
UNAVEM I United Nations Angola Verification Mission I
UNTAG United Nations Transition Assistance Group
ONUCA United Nations Observer Group in Central America
UNAVEM II United Nations Angola Verification Mission II
UNIKOM United Nations Iraq–Kuwait Observer Mission
MINURSO United Nations Mission for the Referendum in Western Sahara
ONUSA United Nations Observer Mission in El Salvador
UNAMIC United Nations Advanced Mission in Cambodia
UNTAC United Nations Transitional Authority in Cambodia
UNPROFOR United Nations Protection Force in Yugoslavia
ONUMOZ United Nations Mission in Mozambique
UNOSOM I United Nations Operation in Somalia
UNOSOM II United Nations Operation in Somalia II
UNOMUR United Nations Observer Mission in Uganda–Rwanda
UNAMIR United Nations Mission in Rwanda
UNOMIL United Nations Observer Mission in Liberia
UNOMIG United Nations Observer Mission in Georgia
UNMIH United Nations Mission in Haiti
UNOMSA United Nations Observer Mission in South Africa

# INDEX

Numbers in **bold** indicate subjects shown
in pictures as well as in the text.

Afghanistan 26
Aidid, General 53–5
Albania 38
Angola **26**, 28, 30–1
Attlee, Clement 7
Axis Powers 9

Balkans 38, 45
Barre, Siad 48–9
blue berets 7, 16, 53
Bosnia **36**, 37–41, **42**, 43–7, 60
Bosnian Muslims 37–9, **40**, **42**, 44–5
Boutros-Ghali, Boutros 36, 38, 41, 53, **57**
Britain 6, 8, 14, 17, 27, 43
Bulgaria 38

Cambodia 33, **34–5**
Carter, Jimmy 45
China 8–9, 11, 23, 27
Clinton, Bill 55
Cold War **8**, 9–10, 12, 15–16, 24–6, 56–7,
    60
Communism 28, 36
Congo 20, 53
Croatia 37, **38–9**
Croats 41–2, 44–5, 47
Cuellar, Perez de **26–8**, **60**
Cyprus 57–8, **59**
Czechoslovakia 25

Egypt **17–20**, 21, **22**
Empire of Austria–Hungary 37
enforcement of peace 8, 10, 15
ethnic cleansing 39

First World War 37
France 8, 14, **17**, 27, 36, **41**

Gaza Strip **18**
Germany 9, 14, 28
Golan Heights 22–4
Gorazde 37, 43
Gorbachev, Mikhail 26
Greece 38, 59
Gulf War 10, 12–13, **14–15**

Hammarskjold, Dag 16
Horn of Africa 48
Hungary **25**

Iran 13–14
Iraq 13, **14–15**, **23**, 24
Israel 17, **18–19**, **21**, 22–3, **24**
Italy 9, 55

Japan 9, 14

Kampuchea, see Cambodia
Kashmir **16**
Khmer Rouge 34, **35**, 53
Korean War **10**, 11–12, 15
Kuwait 13–14, **15**

League of Nations 28

Macedonia 37–8, 46
Middle East 16–17, 25
Mogadishu 49, **52**, 53
Montenegro 37, **43**

Namibia **27**, 28–9, **30**, 31, **32**, 36
Nasser 17
Nationalist China 8–9, 23
NATO 10, 43–5

observer forces
    nature of 20
Operation Desert Storm 10, **12**, **14**

Pakistani peacekeepers 50–1, 53
People's Republic of China 11, 27
Pol Pot 34

Red Sea 49
Russia (see also Soviet Union) 13–15, 27,
    46, 58

Sadat, Anwar 21
SADF 30, **31**
Sarajevo **36–7**, 41, **42**, **44–5**, 47
Saudi Arabia 14
Second World War 9, 11, 36
Security Council **7**, 9–10, 13–15, **23**, 26–7,
    41–2, **43**, 49, **50**, 53, 57
    permanent members 9
Serbia 37–9, 41, **43**
Serbs 37–8, **42**–7, 53
Sinai 18, **19**
Six-Day War 19, **20**

Slovenia 37
Somalia 20, 46, **48**, 49, **50–55**, 60
    problems of UN in 55
South Africa 27–9, **31**
South West Africa 28
Soviet Union (see also Russia) 6, **8**, 11–12,
    14–15, 21, **25**, 26–7, 34, 36
Suez crisis 16, **17**
SWAPO 28, 30–31, **33**
SWAPOL 32
Syria 20–23, **24**

Tito, Marshal 36
Truman, Harry S. **6–7**
Turkey 14, 59
Turkish Empire 37
Turkish Republic of North Cyprus 59

UN
    Charter 49
    founding of **6**, 8
    headquarters **6**, **56**
    peacekeeping role
        difficulties of 25, 55
        financial contributions to 26, 57–8
        future of 60
        nature of 7, 19–20

UN General Assembly **6**,9, **56**
UNDOF 21–22, **24**, 25
UNEF 16–18, **19**, 20–22, 25
UNHCR **40**, 43
UNIFICYP 58, **59**
Unita 53
UNITAF **50**, 51, **52**
UNOSOM I 50, **51**
UNOSOM II, 52, **54**, 55
UNPROFOR 36, **38–40**, 41–2, 44–5, 47
UNTAC 34–5
UNTAG **27**, **30**, 31–3
USA 8, **10–12**, 13–15, 21, 25, 27, 51, **53**,
    54, 57–8

veto, use in Security Council of 9, 12
Vietnam 25, 34

Warsaw Pact 10

*Yom Kippur* War 20, **21**, 22
Yugoslavia **19**, 36–7, 45

Zaire (see Congo)
Zambia 30